BRIAN JOHNSTON

Putting the Gospel First

A Bible Study of the Book of Romans

HAYES
PRESS Christian Publisher

First edition

This book was professionally typeset on Reedsy. Find out more at reedsy.com

Contents

1	Introduction	1
2	Condemnation	8
3	Justification	15
4	Sanctification	22
5	Glorification	30
6	Predestination	37
7	Transformation	44
8	Conclusion	52
	About the Author	59
	More Books from Brian Johnston	60
	About Hayes Press	63

1

Introduction

God used the Apostle Paul to make a major contribution to the writings that would come to make up the complete Bible - sixty-six books in all, thirteen of them authored by Paul. His letter to the Galatian believers was the first of his letters to be written, some seventeen years after his conversion (and so around AD 50). The writing of this letter connects with his first missionary journey: after Paul had returned back to base at Antioch and before his Jerusalem Council visit. On his second missionary journey, he'd write the two letters to the Thessalonians; and on his third missionary journey he wrote three letters, of which two were to the Corinthians and one to the Romans.

That brings us to Paul's letter to the Romans. Although not the first to be written, it has first place in the order in which we find Paul's writings in the New Testament listing of Bible books. So, in that sense it's brought forward, as it were, pushed to the forefront. It's this that's given us the title of this book - "Putting the Gospel First." Lots, perhaps all, of Paul's other letters were concerned in a more major way with fighting fires – that is, with correcting serious difficulties that had arisen in the very first churches of God in the first century. It's sobering to think of the problems that existed in those churches. But, in one sense, we might even say it was good that these churches were so imperfect because these problems gave the impetus for the rich teaching Paul poured into the letters he wrote to them. There's not only the clarity of the correction that was administered, but above all it's the way Christ gets exalted in marvellous sections of these writings by Paul.

Among his letters, Paul urges his readers to have a mentality that was suited to their identity – their new identity in Christ (Colossians 3:1,2). He encourages them to set their minds on things much higher than the mundane things of this life. Their focus was to be on heaven's throne where Christ had taken his seat upon his ascension, after being raised from the dead. From the first Christian sermon preached by the Apostle Peter, we see how this thought of the enthroned and exalted Christ had gripped the first Christians (Acts 2:33). It's worth pausing at that thought to ask: 'Where do my thoughts wander to when my mind is not having to engage with other practical matters?'

When you read Paul's letters, it's clear that his thoughts always escaped to the Gospel. The Good News of what God has done for us through Christ at the cross was the passion of his life. How fitting, then, that whereas Galatians was the first letter to be written chronologically, the letter to the Romans with its Gospel content is the first of Paul's letters that we encounter canonically – that is, it's first in order as we find them presented in our Bibles.

Even if you're already familiar with the Gospel of Jesus Christ whom Paul preached, I glad you're joining me for these studies as we follow Paul's expert and Spirit-filled defence of the Gospel. He'll soon be standing for the defence of the Gospel before Caesar's tribunal at the heart of the Empire, but here in the pages of his letter to the Romans – pages in which he anticipates his visit there – he already sets out for all time such a wonderfully orderly defence of the Gospel that it squarely faces up to, and systematically defeats, every conceivable objection to it.

It has been remarked by others that there are eight main sections to this letter, so I'll make use of them. We start now with the first of the eight; that is, with the Introduction (that occupies Romans chapter one, verses one through seventeen). Before we come to the text itself, perhaps it's worth sharing a historical note by way of introduction to this great letter. It's one that demonstrates how God's Word as found in this letter has transformed the lives of countless men and women down through the centuries since Paul wrote it.

We start then with the true story about the spiritual crisis that assailed a professor of literature struggling to live down his turbulent past. The preaching of Ambrose had brought him to conviction and, unable to find rest, he went out into the sunshine of his back garden in Milan, Italy. Under a tree he was breaking his heart when he heard some children playing outside, chanting a little song: "pick up and read ..." Wondering if this could be the answer for him, he picked up the Bible which happened to be lying handy and read from Romans 13. The words he read (from verse 11) were these: *"not in riots and drunken parties ..."* it said but *"... put on the Lord Jesus Christ."* And that was how the famous Augustine got saved in the year AD 386.

Nearly 1,200 years later, this time in Germany, a monk of the order of that same Augustine was undergoing his very own spiritual crisis. Regarding this letter to the Romans he said: "Night and day I thought over it until ... I understood that the righteousness of God is of such a nature that he justifies us by grace and mercy through faith. Upon that I felt I was reborn and had entered Paradise through an open door." The name of this man who entered through that open door - the door, so to speak, of Romans 1 verse 17 - was Martin Luther. And, of course, within 2 years - in 1517 - he, in turn, opened the door on the Protestant Reformation.

Then, on the eve of 24 May, 1738, John Wesley went "very unwillingly" to a Moravian meeting in the Aldersgate Street where someone was reading Luther's foreword to the letter to the Romans. "At about quart[er] to 9 while hearing about the change God works in our heart through faith in Christ," Wesley would later acknowledge, "I found my (own) heart strangely warmed. I felt I trusted on Christ alone for salvation" - and he received the assurance that his sins were taken away. And so began the 18th century English Revival which historians note had a profound effect upon the country at large! And so there we have an interlocking chain of events in which Paul's letter to the Romans changed influential lives down through history – as it has done for countless others, of course.

Well, we should introduce the text of the Bible now using Paul's own introduction to his letter to Rome. At both the introduction and at the conclusion of his letter to the Romans, Paul uses the expression "the obedience of faith." Please make no mistake about it: faith that's real will produce obedience. Here's how Paul opens his letter to the Romans:

> *"Paul, a bond-servant of Christ Jesus, called as an apostle, set apart for the gospel of God, which He promised beforehand through His prophets in the holy Scriptures, concerning His Son, who was born of a descendant of David according to the flesh, who was declared the Son of God with power by the resurrection from the dead, according to the Spirit of holiness, Jesus Christ our Lord, through whom we have received grace and apostleship to bring about the obedience of faith among all the Gentiles for His name's sake ..."* (Romans 1:1-5).

The Gospel is the Gospel of God concerning his son. It's divine as to its author and subject. But I want you to particularly notice there the mention of *"the obedience of faith."* This was the goal of Paul's preaching – and that of the other apostles. Such a thing as "easy believe-ism" – "just believe" – wasn't known to Paul. That wasn't the essence of Paul's preaching. The Gospel, once accepted, should shape our whole life. True faith is obedience involving surrender, repentance, commitment and submission to the authority or Lordship of Jesus Christ.

Bible scholars (e.g. Robertson) inform us that this is describing the obedience that springs from faith (and not describing obedience to faith). Another (Vincent) agrees and adds: "the obedience of faith is the obedience which characterizes and proceeds from faith." The point is: real faith is characterized by nothing less than obedience. *"The obedience of faith"* is our yielding ourselves to belief in God's saving message, which is the highest of all obedience. Yielding to the message and surrendering to Christ. Faith, self-renouncing trust in Jesus Christ, is obedience to the gospel command to believe on the Lord Jesus Christ for salvation - and that faith in Jesus Christ initiates a believer into a life of obedience to Jesus Christ.

Faith is no mere notional or mental assent to biblical propositions. Real faith always has works of obedience. The great Reformers would tell us: it's faith alone that saves, but the faith that saves us is never alone – it's never without obedience to the lordship of Christ our saviour.

We should allow the Apostle Paul the last word in introducing his letter on the fundamental truths of the Christian message or Gospel: *"For I am not ashamed of the gospel, for it is the power of God for salvation to everyone who believes, to the Jew first and also to the Greek. For in it the righteousness of God is revealed from faith to faith; as it is written: " But the righteous one will live by faith"* (Romans 1:16,17).

Having revisited there the verse that God used to bring conviction to the heart of Martin Luther, we bring this introduction to the Bible letter to the Romans to a close.

Questions for Further Study

1. Which 'Gospel' promises can you identify in the Old Testament – promises that signalled in advance something of what was going to be revealed fully in the New Testament (v.2)?

2. Can we be saved (forgiven of all sins) without any obedience (v.5)? Why or why not?
3. How is both the righteousness and the wrath of God revealed (vv.17,18)?
4. We often lead up to a presentation of the Gospel today by employing an 'apologetics' approach. What evidence for God's existence does Paul assert (vv.19,20)?

2

Condemnation

As I write this, the news headline has been about three men, two of them British, who have been condemned to death on charges of terrorism, having been convicted of fighting with the Ukrainian resistance against Russian forces. And condemnation is the theme of the first major section of the Apostle Paul's letter to the Romans (1:18-3:20). This section, themed on Condemnation, stretches roughly from the middle of chapter one and reaches all the way until we get to the middle of chapter three.

The imagery that I once read being used to describe this section has never left me. Picture a condemned man in his cell listening to the pounding footsteps of the executioner getting closer and closer, sounding ever nearer until the cell door is flung open. Shall we listen to some of the pounding footsteps of that approaching executioner?

> *"For the wrath of God is revealed from heaven against all ungodliness ... For even though they knew God, they*

did not honor Him as God or give thanks ... Therefore God gave them up to vile impurity in the lusts of their hearts, so that their bodies would be dishonored among them. For they exchanged the truth of God for falsehood ... For this reason God gave them over to degrading passions; ... receiving in their own persons the due penalty of their error. And just as they did not see fit to acknowledge God, God gave them up to a depraved mind ... and although they know the ordinance of God, that those who practice such things are worthy of death, they not only do the same, but also approve of those who practice them" (Romans 1:18-32).

It's relentless. And as we move into the second chapter, there's no escape for Jew as well as Gentile:

"Therefore you have no excuse, you foolish person, everyone of you who passes judgment; for in that matter in which you judge someone else, you condemn yourself; for you who judge practice the same things. And we know that the judgment of God rightly falls upon those who practice such things ... There will be tribulation and distress for every soul of mankind who does evil, for the Jew first and also for the Greek, but glory, honor, and peace to everyone who does what is good, to the Jew first and also to the Greek. For there is no partiality with God. For all who have sinned without the Law will also perish without the Law, and all who have sinned under the Law will be judged by the Law ..." (Romans 2:1-12).

This is where it becomes totally clear that even God's chosen people of the Old Testament are far from immune to these judgements. Paul continues: *"You who boast in the Law, through your breaking the Law, do you dishonor God? For 'the name of God is blasphemed among the Gentiles because of you,' just as it is written?"* (Romans 2:23,24). It's now made crystal clear that all the world is guilty.

> *"Their condemnation is deserved. What then? Are we better than they? Not at all; for we have already charged that both Jews and Greeks are all under sin; as it is written:*
>   *"There is no righteous person, not even one;*
>   *There is no one who understands,*
>   *There is no one who seeks out God;*
>   *They have all turned aside, together they have become corrupt;*
>   *There is no one who does good,*
>   *There is not even one"* (Romans 3:8-12).

At this point, the condemnation is complete and universal. It is without exception. All humanity is guilty before its holy creator God. It's here that we might imagine the handle of the cell door to turn and the door to swing open to give access to the executioner who has come at last to carry out the sentence. But instead, when the door swings open, as it were, it appears as if light suddenly streams into our darkened cell!

> *"Now we know that whatever the Law says, it speaks to those who are under the Law, so that every mouth may be closed and all the world may become accountable to God; because by the works of the Law none of mankind will be justified in His sight; for through the Law comes*

knowledge of sin. But now apart from the Law the
righteousness of God has been revealed, being witnessed
by the Law and the Prophets, but it is the righteousness of
God through faith in Jesus Christ for all those who believe;
for there is no distinction" (Romans 3:19-22).

Having given us the bad news first, detailing our universal and inexcusable state of condemnation as guilty sinners exposed to the righteous wrath of a holy God, suddenly hope appears! It is accessed by faith in Christ alone. This is cause for such celebration that I want to jump ahead and quote from a later verse (Romans 5:11): *"And not only this, but we also celebrate in God through our Lord Jesus Christ, through whom we have now received the reconciliation."*

As the song many of us sing at Christmas-time says: "God and sinners reconciled." The idea behind and within this word is the idea of an exchange. Think of a typical human situation where two former friends have become alienated from each other due to some misunderstanding. If they can work through their problems and resolve them then they exchange their enmity or hatred for peace. It's that exchange of attitude that's at the root of their reconciliation with each other. But the message of Romans is about our becoming reconciled to God. And we've been reading of the need for that in terms of the anger of a holy God that burns against the sin of our rebelliousness against him.

Reconciliation, with its idea of two things being exchanged, is a big word in the Christian Good News message. If I may, I would like to broaden things out at this point and say more generally that there are at least five exchanges that are involved as we try to understand first the bad news and then the good news - the good news of God's remedy for the human condition. While Paul was exposing the human condition for us, he literally talked about how we exchanged God's truth for falsehood (Romans 1:25). So, that's the first of the exchanges that I have in mind – and it's one exchange that goes to the very root of the problem faced by all of us, without distinction, as Paul says.

Its effect was also made clear by Paul in the quotes we read from the first 3 chapters of this letter to the Romans we're looking at. And that effect was to bring us – that's the whole world – under God's condemnation. That, of course, wasn't the initial condition of humanity when God created us in his image. No, we were designed for fellowship with our creator God. But when we exchanged God's truth for falsehood, then instantly the communion that we humans had known with our creator was exchanged for condemnation. The word "condemnation" certainly appears in the Bible text at this point (Romans 3:8). More than that, it is the theme of this section of Paul's letter, and that's the reason, of course, for using it as the title of this chapter.

Although the Apostle Paul doesn't mention the first man, Adam, by name until later in chapter five, the first two exchanges we've already talked about – those of God's truth for falsehood and communion being exchanged for our condemnation before God – can be traced back to the action of the first man, the first responsible head of the human race. But at the point where we imagined the door of our condemned cell bursting open, a different name was introduced - that of Jesus Christ. In another place, the Apostle Paul describes him as *"the last Adam"* (1

Corinthians 15:45). And so the glory of the Gospel preached by Paul begins to unfold. Just as Adam stands at the head of a race of condemned humanity, so Jesus Christ now stands at the head of new humanity, being all those who are made righteous in him.

Yes, this exchange of Christ being now in the place of Adam introduces us to the most glorious truth of all - and utterly central to the Christian message - and it's simply this: that our sinful standing as one belonging to Adam can be exchanged for our righteous standing as believers who belong instead to Jesus Christ. We will see in our next study that, at the cross where he died bearing our guilt before a holy God, Christ took upon himself the legal consequences of our sin that we might receive his righteousness in exchange. That, I believe, is what Martin Luther called "the great exchange."

There we have two more exchanges: Christ for Adam and, as a result, righteousness for sin. But how does it become effective in the case of each one of us personally? Ah well, I'll have to conclude this chapter by saying that is the result of exchange number five: the exchange of belief for unbelief. We give up all dependence on our own good works for faith alone is instrumental for all these exchanges.

Questions for Further Study

1. 'Gospel' means 'Good News'. What do you find towards the end of Romans ch.1 that sets out the need for such good news (vv.21–32)?

2. How would you reply to someone who misunderstood Romans 2:7,8 as implying a person who does good things will be saved from God's judgement; whereas selfish and unjust persons will subjected to God's wrath in the resurrection? (Hint: does it help to think of how things may be correlated without being linked by 'cause and effect'?)
3. Can you pick out verses that show Jews are just as much in need of God's salvation as Gentiles?
4. Did you manage to pinpoint exactly the verse at which, as it were, the condemned cell door suddenly opens with undeserved and totally surprising good news?

3

Justification

In this chapter I'd like us to examine our third topic - and our third section - from chapter 3:21 to chapter 5:21 in the Apostle Paul's letter to the Romans. It's the reversal of condemnation and that's justification. If condemnation is about us being declared guilty before a holy God whom we've offended by our rebellious attitude and behaviour against him, then justification is about us being declared righteous before God. It's about having a right standing before him, a right relationship with him.

I just love how systematic the Apostle Paul is as the Spirit leads him in such an orderly way through these great themes of the Gospel. Not only do they follow on the one from the other, but as we come to look at Justification, we'll see how Paul tackles it by first setting out its **Instruction** (Romans 3:21-26); and then its **Implications** (Romans 3:27-31); and finally, its **Illustrations** (chapters 4 & 5 dealing with Abraham and Adam).

But even within each of these three sub-headings, we find further structured treatments. Let's take the first – the instruction in chapter 3 verses 21–26 that he gives us about this great Gospel word of justification. This is surely the most concise description of what God did for us through his son, Jesus Christ, and did it all supremely at the cross. The words that follow are simply packed with vital instruction:

> *"But now apart from the Law the righteousness of God has been revealed, being witnessed by the Law and the Prophets, but it is the righteousness of God through faith in Jesus Christ for all those who believe; for there is no distinction, for all have sinned and fall short of the glory of God, being justified as a gift by His grace through the redemption which is in Christ Jesus, whom God displayed publicly as a propitiation in His blood through faith. This was to demonstrate His righteousness, because in God's merciful restraint He let the sins previously committed go unpunished; for the demonstration, that is, of His righteousness at the present time, so that He would be just and the justifier of the one who has faith in Jesus."*

In the briefest of summaries, we could say here is a salvation that is apart from Law, witnessed by the Old Testament (v.21); provided by God (v.22a); received by faith (v.22b); needed by all (v.23); given by grace (v.24a); purchased by Jesus (v.24b); and both declared and designed by God (vv.25,26). What a salvation is ours!

The amazing thing is at verse 21 it's as if the key turns in the lock and the door to the prison cell swings open. This is the prison holding condemned sinners, but when the door finally opens

- instead of the executioner standing there – light floods into the prisoner's cell with the bright news of a pardon and with release papers for him to sign. All that preceded this gave no reason to expect it. The bad news suddenly turns to good news (i.e. "Gospel") at this point. How is this possible? The answer lies in what we've just read.

When Paul speaks of *"righteousness of God through faith in Jesus Christ"* (Romans 3:22), he means a "right standing" before God, one that God himself gives to sinners. And no distinction exists between sinners, whether Jew or Gentile - all are exposed to God's wrath on account of sin. But, more wonderfully, there's also no human distinction as to who may be justified either, because the right standing before God that's suddenly announced is a gift that's all of God's grace!

When a God like this saves us by placing us in a right standing before him, he does it in accordance with what's right. Both the righteousness God gives to us, and the righteousness that's his own, are relevant. God's own righteousness was demonstrated at the cross (Romans 3:25,26). Since in his forbearance he'd not always in the past punished sinners immediately, there was the possibility that God might be thought not to be just (Romans 3:25). But no longer.

When we read the words *"the righteousness of God through faith in Jesus Christ for all those who believe"* in verse 22, it's worth thinking carefully about whose faith or faithfulness is first mentioned there. Is it ours or Christ's? It avoids repetition and it's quite grammatical to see Christ as the subject, rather than the object, of the faith first mentioned in verse 22. In other words, it's Christ's faith – or his faithfulness [same word – *pistis*]. Paul sees the works of the Law being replaced with what they pointed forward to; namely, the faithful work of Christ.

To justify someone is to declare him or her as "not guilty"; in fact, more positively, it's to declare us to be righteous in God's sight. Christ paid the penalty due to all those who are declared to be righteous.

Let's now turn with Paul from the language of the law-courts to the language of the temple- shrines, and look into the word "propitiation" or "atoning sacrifice." As well as being found here, it's used in the Bible (see Hebrews 9:5) to describe the mercy seat which acted as a covering lid for the Old Testament ark of the covenant. The mercy seat is especially associated with the Day of Atonement (or the "day of propitiation" LXX). There in God's presence, stained annually with the blood of sacrifice, and under the gaze of the cherubim which were part of its design, the mercy seat stood as witness to the fact that justice was satisfied. God had not ignored sin but the price of justice had been met in blood.

The word "propitiation" (*hilasterion*, Romans 3:25) then pictures for us the removal of wrath, as when pagans would appease their upset gods by offering them sweet-meats. But compared with its pagan background, its Bible use is radically different in terms of who initiates it - who provides the offering - and in understanding God's anger against sin to be far from the fickle upset of pagan gods! The Greeks had made gods in their own human image with petty insecurities and jealousies. Coming to the New Testament, we find no room for pagan thinking. God's wrath is the unalterable holy antagonism of the unchangeable God towards sin. It's not men who interpose with gifts to appease God, but it's God himself who intervenes to send his own son for the sacrificial work of the cross. It's this that defines love: *"This is love, not that we have loved God but that he loved us and sent his Son to be the propitiation for our sins"* (1 John 4:10). Divine wrath was completely satisfied by the covering work of Christ for all those who are united with Christ by faith.

If "justification" – to declare as righteous – is the language of the law-court; and "propitiation" is the language of the temple-shrine, then "redemption" – meaning to buy back or set free – is the language of the slave-market in which humans are pictured as slaves to sin. It's also used here to give us full instruction about how God can himself be just while also be the one who justifies freely all who put their full trust in Christ alone.

Well, so much for the instruction about justification which Paul has given us as he explains exactly how God is able to declare as righteous those who were previously condemned as sinners. Paul now turns to the implications of this justification in vv.27-31...

> *"Where then is boasting? It has been excluded. By what kind of law? Of works? No, but by a law of faith. For we maintain that a person is justified by faith apart from works of the Law. Or is God the God of Jews only? Is He not the God of Gentiles also? Yes, of Gentiles also, since indeed God who will justify the circumcised by faith and the uncircumcised through faith is one. Do we then nullify the Law through faith? Far from it! On the contrary, we*

establish the Law."

I like to remember those three implications as being respectively: no boasting, no barriers, and no banishing (meaning to say the moral law has not been banished). God's way of justifying sinners totally excludes us from boasting about ourselves. But, instead, we are left boasting only about God. This is the same word used three times in Romans chapter 5 where it's translated as "celebrate" ...

> *"Therefore, having been justified by faith, we have peace with God ... and we celebrate in hope of the glory of God. And not only this, but we also celebrate in our tribulations, knowing that tribulation brings about perseverance; and perseverance, proven character; and proven character, hope; and hope does not disappoint, because the love of God has been poured out within our hearts through the Holy Spirit who was given to us. For while we were still helpless, at the right time Christ died for the ungodly ... And not only this, but we also celebrate in God through our Lord Jesus Christ, through whom we have now received the reconciliation."*

It's very clear that we have no boasting in ourselves but only cause to celebrate or boast in God. Now, let's come to what we said was "no barriers" in God's way of justifying sinners. This was emphasized by repeating that God is not only the God of Jews. Circumcision is mentioned as characterising the Jew, but as Paul adds in chapter 4:9-11 ... *"Faith was credited to Abraham as righteousness ... Not while circumcised, but while uncircumcised ... so that he might be the father of all who believe without being circumcised.*" So, no boasting and no barriers in God's way of justifying sinners. But finally, it's also done in a way that doesn't banish God's moral law.

"God ... sending His own Son in the likeness of sinful flesh and as an offering for sin ... condemned sin in the flesh, so that the requirement of the Law might be fulfilled in us who do not walk according to the flesh but according to the Spirit" (Romans 8:3,4). This introduces us to the illustrations of justification featuring Abraham and Adam.

Questions for Further Study

1. How would you sum up what the Gospel is, in your own words?
2. How would you explain how God can both be just himself and at the same time justify those who put their trust in Jesus (v.26)?
3. In what ways does the pagan religious 'appeasing' of god(s) differ from the work of the cross and the atoning sacrifice of Jesus Christ?
4. What kind of 'boasting' is excluded for the Christian and what other kind of 'boasting' (celebration) replaces it?

4

Sanctification

The fourth section of the Apostle Paul's letter to the Romans that we now come to study is the one we're entitling "Sanctification." We'll come to see this has two parts - in one sense it's already complete in Christ; but for the other part it's an ongoing process in Christian living. Paul's treatment of this topic of sanctification takes us from the beginning of chapter 6 right through to about halfway down chapter 8. The start of chapter 6 is clearly dealing with sanctification – that is, holiness – because here Paul is responding to those who were objecting by saying: "we might as well go on sinning if we're already assured of God's forgiveness!"

Although this topic starts at chapter 6, its roots go back to where we've already been studying. Perhaps, then, it's worthwhile to make a couple of linking observations from chapters 4 and 5. This will allow us to catch up with the two illustrations we anticipated from our previous study. First, in chapter 4, our attention has just got to be grabbed by the repetitive use of the word "credited" (Logizomai – to credit, count, reckon, impute).

It occurs 5 times within 9 verses (vv.3-11). To credit someone means "to put something in someone's account" (e.g. Philemon v.18).

God took Abraham star-gazing one day when he was already an old, childless man, and told him that his descendants would be as numerous as the stars. Against all the odds, Abraham believed God's word to him and this faith was "credited to him" as righteousness. To impute righteousness is to set righteousness to someone's account and to treat him accordingly; whereas, of course, to impute sin is to lay sin to the charge of someone and to treat him accordingly (C.H. Hodge). It's helpful to get a secure grasp of those two credits into our account because they link together the two illustrations Paul draws out from the lives of Abraham and Adam.

We're talking, of course, about Adam, the very first human. The doctrine of the imputation of Adam's sin means that when Adam first sinned, that sin (and its blame) was regarded by God to be our sin as well. It counted against us. Adam's sin became our sin and his judgment became our judgment. Beginning at Romans 5:12, Paul teaches that we all sinned *in Adam* when *"through one man sin entered into the world."* He adds (vv.13-14) that while people sinned personally in the time before Moses, their personal sins were not the ultimate reason why people died in that time period. These personal sins were not imputed to them (or counted against them) because back then there was no law: *"sin is not imputed when there is no law."*

The actual reason they died was because they'd all sinned in Adam. That is, they'd not personally "sinned in the likeness of the offense of Adam" simply because they didn't sin against a known and understood law or command (as Adam had done). We learn from this that death is not first and foremost because of our own individual sinning, but because of our (corporate) union with Adam, the federal head of the human race. His sin was credited to our account.

To underline this point, in vv.15-18, Paul says no less than four times that *"death and condemnation"* comes upon all humans because of *"the one transgression of the one man."* We are identified with Adam such that his one sin is regarded as our sin and we are worthy of condemnation for it. This is the *"sin of the world"* that would be taken away by the Lamb of God (John 1:29). To sum it up, Paul says in verse 19, *"Through the one man's disobedience the many were made sinners."* This is talking very plainly about how Adam's one original sin counts against us all.

Adam is the only person in the Bible explicitly declared to be a "type" or "prophetic symbol" of Christ (v.14). Never dismiss the Old Testament; the grandeur of the Gospel takes us right the way back to the Bible's first book and to history's very first character. Whereas Adam walked in disobedience to the tree and his sin counted against us all; Christ walked in perfect obedience to the tree where he took away that sin of the world. That which had entered the world through Adam and (the guilt thereof) was taken away by the last Adam - for all. This is the singular sin of the world, relating to the root sinful condition of humanity as per the biblical doctrine of original sin.

We now come to Romans chapter 6, and just as in Romans 5:12 where "sin" is quite literally "the sin," we find it's the same as we go into Romans 6 where it's strictly speaking "the sin" that continues to be mentioned (e.g. in vv.2,7). Speaking of Christian believers, Paul says that in Adam we sinned to death; but in the last Adam (who is Christ), we died to (the) sin. Specifically, following on seamlessly from chapter 5 this seems to be a reference to the dead root of our sin nature. We may view it as withering away yet still capable of bad fruit, but since we now possess a new nature (and since we're now a new person) in Christ, we need no longer to be mastered by it, but rather we should be the one mastering it.

And this is precisely where our sanctification comes into focus. The end of chapter 5 sees sin reigning as king (Romans 5:21). Sin is personified, since it reigns as king, and this can only be referring to the evil nature still resident in the Christian, as we've thought. The logical argument of Romans chapter 6 that follows on from this is: that sin should no longer reign as king in our mortal body such that we obey its lusts (v.12). This is because the Christian believer, seen in union with Christ, is counted by God as having already actually died with Christ – so that our body of (the) sin might be made powerless (v.6).

We've been *"freed from* (the) *sin"* (v.18), but we're not free from the effects of our fallen nature. Even before Adam sinned, human freedom was not absolute liberty – for that can only be true of God. God is the only being who is not influenced by anything outside of himself. In contrast, God's dependent creatures can only, in the nature of things, have limited freedom – even if real.

Adam's sin was, or it at very least involved, the desire to increase

25

his real freedom to be absolute freedom like that of the creator. Sadly, things went in the opposite direction for our freedom is now additionally without the moral ability to choose for good or for God.

Adam before the Fall had both the ability to sin and the ability to not sin. After the Fall, the moral condition of original sin that applies to us all is tragically the **inability** to not sin. That's not to say we've lost freewill. After the Fall, we still have a will that's free in the sense that it is not coerced by any external agency. We still have the ability to make choices according to our own desires; but now, however, the human will is in a state of corruption. We are still free to do what we want, but the problem lies in what we want. In Adam, we lost any innate desire to seek for, and to please, God. We lack the freedom to do, or choose, good as well as evil. Our freedom was never absolute, but additionally, we're now in bondage to our corrupted nature.

The big issue is how a person can regain liberty - the moral ability to choose what's good, to choose the things of God. Since fallen man is spiritually dead, he's a slave to himself, to his passions and lusts; he follows the desires of his evil heart. This is the Lord's teaching in John 8 when he taught the disbelieving Jews that the truth would make them free (v.32). Like so many today, they did not see themselves as anything other than free or as anything other than basically good. The Lord told them *"everyone who commits sin is the slave of sin"* (v.34). The liberation of fallen humanity absolutely requires God's grace – *"if the Son makes you free, you will be free indeed"* (v.36).

The teaching of sanctification that's found in Romans chapters

6 through 8, is that we, who are believers in Christ, are not the persons we once were. We – that is, our old self, our old persona – died with Christ. We died to sin in the death of Christ. As a result, sin is no longer king of our lives; but Jesus is our Lord - he's now the king of our lives. Having died to it, we're freed from sin. But at the same time, we're not free to please ourselves. No, we've become slaves to righteousness. Everybody has to serve somebody. Paul says so here - a person is either a slave to sin or a slave to righteousness.

Just as God counts us as having died to sin in the death of Christ, we're to count (that same word again!) ourselves as dead to sin day by day. The first part of that is what God does: our once for all sanctification (1 Corinthians 6:11; Hebrews 10:10). The second part is what's our daily responsibility (Hebrews 12:10-14). This is what Paul sees as being our duty:

"Consider yourselves to be dead to sin, but alive to God in Christ Jesus. Therefore sin is not to reign in your mortal body so that you obey its lusts, and do not go on presenting the parts of your body to sin as instruments of unrighteousness; but present yourselves to God as those who are alive from the dead, and your body's parts as instruments of righteousness for God. For sin shall not be master over you, for you are not under the Law but under grace.

What then? Are we to sin because we are not under the Law but under grace? Far from it! Do you not know that the one to whom you present yourselves as slaves for obedience, you are slaves of that same one whom

27

you obey, either of sin resulting in death, or of obedience resulting in righteousness? But thanks be to God that though you were slaves of sin, you became obedient from the heart to that form of teaching to which you were entrusted" (Romans 6:11-17).

The full logic of this chapter is: 'you're not the person you once were therefore don't live as you once lived!' But that's hard to do in our own strength. Worse than that - it's impossible. For Paul himself illustrates that in chapter 7 where he admits ...

"I am not practicing what I want to do, but I do the very thing I hate ... But now, no longer am I the one doing it, but sin that dwells in me. For I know that good does not dwell in me, that is, in my flesh; for the willing is present in me, but the doing of the good is not. For the good that I want, I do not do, but I practice the very evil that I do not want. But if I do the very thing I do not want, I am no longer the one doing it, but sin that dwells in me" (Romans 7:15-20).

This problem of indwelling sin can only be overcome by the help of the indwelling Spirit of God. Then we arrive at the point where we can say *"that the requirement of the Law might be fulfilled in us who do not walk according to the flesh but according to the Spirit"* (Romans 8:4).

Questions for Further Study

1. In what way does the Gospel narrative and its result for us depend on the historical Adam?
2. In what way(s) is Adam a 'prophetic symbol' of Christ; and how are we to understand Jesus as being 'the last Adam'?
3. Try to put into your own words what it means to be 'counted a sinner' due to being 'in Adam'; and 'counted righteous' due to being found by grace to be 'in Christ'? Does either require any work on our part?
4. How does this section support both the 'once-for-all' and 'work-in-progress' aspects of our sanctification (our being made holy)?

5

Glorification

Having dealt with Condemnation, Justification and then Sanctification in our previous studies of the Gospel, as we work our
way through the Apostle Paul's letter to the Romans, we now
come to Glorification. Let's enjoy a section of chapter 8 - from
verse 28 until the end:

> *"And we know that God causes all things to work together
> for good to those who love God, to those who are called
> according to His purpose. For those whom He foreknew,
> He also predestined to become conformed to the image of
> His Son, so that He would be the firstborn among many
> brethren; and these whom He predestined, He also called;
> and these whom He called, He also justified; and these
> whom He justified, He also glorified. What then shall we
> say to these things? If God is for us, who is against us? He
> who did not spare His own Son, but delivered Him over
> for us all, how will He not also with Him freely give us all
> things?*

Who will bring a charge against God's elect? God is the one who justifies; who is the one who condemns? Christ Jesus is He who died, yes, rather who was raised, who is at the right hand of God, who also intercedes for us. Who will separate us from the love of Christ? Will tribulation, or distress, or persecution, or famine, or nakedness, or peril, or sword? Just as it is written, "FOR YOUR SAKE WE ARE BEING PUT TO DEATH ALL DAY LONG; WE WERE CONSIDERED AS SHEEP TO BE SLAUGHTERED." But in all these things we overwhelmingly conquer through Him who loved us" (Romans 8:28-37).

Bible teacher John Stott once pointed out, helpfully I think, that there are really five unshakeable convictions in the first verse we read (verse 28): *"And we know that God causes all things to work together for good to those who love God, to those who are called according to His purpose."*

Paul starts by saying *"we know ..."* Let's explore five things, according to Paul, which we can know about the troubles and difficulties that often intrude into our lives. But, first of all, let's be clear that we're talking about knowing, not understanding. On the basis of what the Bible shares with us in this great verse, we can be convinced about five things. We can have these unshakeable convictions about what's happening to us whenever we encounter trouble and all of a sudden life hurts. And we're going to get to grips with them in a moment, starting with the first of them.

But I really need to emphasize that this kind of knowing is about a certain perspective we can have on the various difficulties of

31

life; but it's not an explanation of why these specific things are happening to us. We may not understand any of the details of God's plan in permitting trouble in our lives. Job, who surely suffered more than anyone else in the whole of the Old Testament, never got to discover the reason why all the evils he suffered started piling up on him. We, the readers, in the comfort of our arm-chair as we read the Bible are let in on the secret – but he never was. He simply learnt to trust in God in the humbling appreciation of glimpsing how much God's wisdom exceeded his own.

So having clarified that let's see what we really can know about what's happening when life hurts, based on God's revelation to us in Romans 8:28. The first thing we learn is: **God is at work in our lives**. When we read: *"God causes all things to work together,"* we should recognize that God is the active subject of the verb. It's the sovereign God who causes the things that happen to us to work together! In reality then, he's the one at work in our lives throughout all the troubles we're facing, unpleasant as they doubtless are. It might feel as if God has turned his back on us and abandoned us. But feelings are very different from faith. This verse teaches us to believe, and so to know, that it is God who is working out his purpose even at difficult times for us.

Which brings us to the second of the five truths in this verse. The first was that God is at work in us. And the second is that **God is at work in us in all things** (vv.17,23). Not just in the good times, but also – and perhaps more so – in the bad times – the times when bad things happen to us. C.S. Lewis put it slightly differently: he said God whispers to us in our pleasures and shouts to us in our pain – pain being his megaphone. Physical pain is a means by which our body warns us against things that can damage us; such as a child learning not to play with fire. To use another analogy, in times of drought trees grow deeper roots in search of water. Later, this experience brings with it the reward of greater stability through a better developed root structure extending throughout the soil. The bad time of drought actually left the tree better equipped to face future storms.

Having explored briefly how God can work out his purpose in our lives in the bad times as well as in the good – and perhaps even more so in those tough experiences – let's hear what the apostle James has to say on this same point: *"Count it all joy, my brothers, when you meet trials of various kinds, for you know that the testing of your faith produces steadfastness. And let steadfastness have its full effect, that you may be perfect and complete, lacking in nothing"* (James 1:2–4).

But we must move on. We've covered two of the five unshakeable convictions hidden like treasure in Romans 8:28. So far, we've seen that God is at work in us at all times. The third point begins to deal with God's intention in allowing his child to pass through such trouble. The verse informs us that **God is at work in us at all times for the good** (vv.29,30) – that is, for our longer-term and future good. We're not expected to fool ourselves into thinking that the present trouble we're passing through is really a good thing in itself. No, for that would be to part company with reality. Trials are, by definition, not pleasant and so not enjoyable. But as James was saying a moment ago in what he wrote in his chapter 1 verses 2 to 4, we can, by God's grace through faith in his Word, come to regard the present difficulty as a "dreaded friend" or even as a "glorious intruder" – to quote two Christians I've met who've passed through life-changing illnesses or accidents. Perhaps the analogy here is the tough time we have at the dentist – it's worth it when we're left free of toothache as a result! In the same way we can pass through challenging growing pains in Christian life as we develop more of the character God desires to see in us, and later we may look back and be satisfied.

The fourth truth is a reminder that God is our loving father and will not cause his child needless pain. It's the Apostle John who says it very plainly when he says that *"everyone who loves is born of God"* (1 John 4:7). So those who love, being God's children, are the ones for whose good God works everything in their lives. For we learn that **God is at work in us in all things for the good of those who love him**. This is a necessary limitation. Verse 28 of Romans 8, from which we're bringing out this teaching, only applies to God's children – to those who have put their faith in Christ and so become his own.

Finally, we learn our fifth truth: that the **God who works in us in all things for our good (that is, the good of those who love him) is the God who called us at the beginning** when we first responded to the Christian good news message and who is continuing to shape us according to his ongoing purpose in us. Everything that happens to us is purposeful if we submit to God's plan. And that ongoing purpose is shared in the very next verse (v.29). But let's read it together with verse 28 which we've been concentrating on thus far:

> *"And we know that for those who love God all things work together for good, for those who are called according to his*

purpose. For those whom he foreknew he also predestined to be conformed to the image of his Son, in order that he might be the firstborn among many brothers" (Romans 8:28-29).

Clearly, it's God's purpose that we should become like his Son, Jesus. That's our destiny. All believers in the world to come will be perfectly like Christ, but God takes great delight in shaping our lives down here – through trials if needed – to reflect more and more the character of the one who entered into his own glories by the pathway of sufferings.

The next verse (v.30) expands on the plan. It's a plan that spans eternity. Some have referred to it as the "Golden chain." It certainly gives confirmation of our eternal security in Christ, and there are four links in this unbreakable chain. The predestined are those who are called -'the called' (1 Corinthians 1:24) - and are again the same as those who are justified, and are also those who will be glorified. The same persons are in view at each stage. It's interesting to note that the final one, glorified, is set in the past tense although it clearly hasn't happened yet. That just goes to show that it's certain to happen, so much so that God treats it as already having taken place. That underlines the fact that no-one who begins this four-stage journey is going to fail to complete it. We are secure in Christ, from eternity to eternity. Not only is Christ to be glorified in us, but we are glorified in Christ (2 Thessalonians 1:12). That's even more remarkable, and is the ultimate display of our sanctification. We will then be as much like Christ as it's possible for created beings to be.

Coming now to verse 32, it's worth noticing that the 'all things' mentioned there are given to exactly those ("us all") for whom Christ was delivered up. This refers back to those already described as predestined, called, justified and glorified. Only those who start off as having been given by the Father to the Son will receive all things. Christ's death will be fully effective for all those for whom it was intended to be so. What comes across here is the grandeur of the God-centred view of our salvation through the Gospel – and even the creation will in future enter the glorious freedom of the children of God (Romans 8:21).

Questions for Further Study

1. What is the longer-term and future good that the sovereign God is working all things together for in our lives (p.29)?
2. What four words sum up God's purpose from eternity to eternity in Christian believers?
3. We've identified 5 'unshakeable convictions' in v.28, how many 'unanswerable (or better, rhetorical) questions' can you find in vv.31-35?
4. This chapter (ch.8) begins with 'no condemnation' (v.1) and concludes with 'no separation' (v.39). Why is it at times that we do not feel like 'overwhelming conquerors' (v.37)?

6

Predestination

As we read through the Bible letter that the Apostle Paul wrote to believers in the Church of God at Rome, we've been tracking through the various sections: Condemnation, Justification, Sanctification, Glorification. That has taken us to the end of chapter 8. For chapters 9 through 11, we have the heading Predestination (or Election).

The escape of the Israelites out of Egypt is one of, if not, *the* main prophetic symbols in all the Bible when it comes to typifying the ultimate deliverance from personal slavery to guilt – a deliverance that God offers us in and through Jesus, his son. If we're at all familiar with the basic storyline of the Old Testament then we can conjure up in our minds the stand-off between Moses and Pharaoh. This was so much more, as the Bible tells us, than the leader of the enslaved people pitting his wits and will against the leader of their oppressors – with both sides invoking their respective deities. At one point God addresses Pharaoh: *"But, indeed, for this reason I have allowed you to remain, in order to show you My power and in order to proclaim My name through all the earth. Still you exalt yourself against My people by not letting them go"* (Exodus 9:16-17). That's how involved God was in this event.

But let's start further back in history, with a woman praying about her difficult pregnancy: *"The LORD said to her, 'Two nations are in your womb; And two peoples will be separated from your body; and one people shall be stronger than the other; and the older shall serve the younger"* (Genesis 25:23).

I think we can assume that Rebekah, the woman in question, shared this revelation with her husband. Isaac, however, seemed partial to his eldest who was an outdoors action figure - a game hunter. He was definitely partial to the food Esau, his eldest, served him. On the other hand, Rebekah's favourite was Jacob. But even if this was because she remembered God's prediction, she didn't seem to believe God could keep his promise without her using her own cunning to give him some assistance. But we're running ahead. The kids haven't even been born yet! Let's go attend the birth ...

> *"When her days to be delivered were fulfilled, behold, there were twins in her womb. Now the first came forth red, all over like a hairy garment; and they named him Esau. Afterward his brother came forth with his hand holding on to Esau's heel, so his name was called Jacob; and Isaac was sixty years old when she gave birth to them"* (Genesis 25:24-26).

It does seem that in his early life Jacob couldn't wait to get his hands on what was his brother's! God had told Rebekah the way things were going to be – with her older son serving his younger brother – and he'd said this not based on their respective early years' performance. (He decreed this before they were even born – so obviously it was quite independent of anything they'd done.) Let's allow the apostle Paul explain it from Romans chapter 9 – he's talking about God's purposes with Israel:

> *"... Rebekah also, when she had conceived* twins *by one man, our father Isaac; for though* the twins *were not yet born and had not done anything good or bad, so that God's purpose according to* His *choice would stand, not because of works but because of Him who calls, it was said to her, "THE OLDER WILL SERVE THE YOUNGER."*

And in case we should think this is an isolated case, as opposed to something illustrating a divine principle, Paul adds our earlier example of the Pharaoh at the time of the Exodus:

> *"What shall we say then? There is no injustice with God, is there? May it never be! For He says to Moses, "I WILL HAVE MERCY ON WHOM I HAVE MERCY, AND I WILL HAVE COMPASSION ON WHOM I HAVE COMPASSION." So then it* does *not depend on the man who wills or the man who runs, but on God who has mercy. For the Scripture says to Pharaoh, "FOR THIS VERY PURPOSE I RAISED YOU UP, TO DEMONSTRATE MY POWER IN YOU, AND THAT MY NAME MIGHT BE PROCLAIMED THROUGHOUT THE WHOLE EARTH"* (Romans 9:10-17).

There's something profound here. We're being allowed some insight into the sovereign workings of God. In this latest Bible example of Pharaoh, king of Egypt, if we were to check back to the book of Exodus and the story of how he refused to give the Israelites their freedom, we'd find that we sometimes read of Pharaoh hardening his own heart and at other times it's said to be God who's hardening his heart – which raises the potential conflict in our minds between divine sovereignty on the one hand and human responsibility on the other. How can we have a real choice if God has already chosen what's going to happen?

Perhaps we could try an analogy here. Even with our modern scientific understanding, in the natural realm there are other things we just can't seem to reconcile. Take the nature of light, for example. There's real evidence that light exists as light waves; some experiments show it to behave in a way comparable to, say, water waves. But, at the same time, there's just as good evidence to show that light and its energy come in little packets, more like particles. The only way we can live with that state of affairs in the natural world is by inventing a name for it. An "antinomy" describes the situation where we have two things which to us are contradictory and yet there's good evidence for both. In a similar way the Bible most definitely teaches both divine sovereignty and human responsibility.

But we tend to shy away from things that are difficult for us to understand – like when it comes to God's involvement in making things happen - and so it's tempting to try to respond to this by saying, "Oh well, God knows in advance what's going to happen and so he can tell us in advance what the future holds." But that doesn't satisfy the language God uses here. Listen to this inspired commentary as Paul continues ...

"So then He has mercy on whom He desires, and He hardens whom He desires. You will say to me then, 'Why does He still find fault? For who resists His will?' On the contrary, who are you, O man, who answers back to God? The thing molded will not say to the molder, 'Why did you make me like this?,' will it? Or does not the potter have a right over the clay, to make from the same lump one vessel for honorable use and another for common use? What if God, although willing to demonstrate His wrath and to make His power known, endured with much patience vessels of wrath prepared for destruction? And He did so *to make known the riches of His glory upon vessels of mercy, which He prepared beforehand for glory ..."* (Romans 9:18-23).

In any case, when the Bible speaks of God knowing the future the word means to know with approval – it's not a passive knowledge, nor can it be, where God is concerned. The question was asked there: "Who resists his will?" In terms of our salvation and eternal destiny, the Bible would fully support that no more than "God wills" to be saved will be saved; but equally, no fewer than the "whosoever wills," will be saved. In other words, no fewer than all who willingly come to Christ for salvation will be saved; but equally, no more than those whom the Father draws to his Son will be saved. It's not something based on any good in us as simply foreseen by God. God's sovereignty includes the fact that Christ's death was effective for all those for whom it was intended to be effective (John 17:9 etc). These receive mercy; while all others receive justice (there being no injustice with God).

So the story of Pharaoh and the Exodus has plunged us into deep water, offering us a glimpse into something very profound. It all demonstrates God's sovereign grace. Paul, by the Spirit of God, has anticipated in that passage from Romans chapter 9 all the questions we want to ask too! For example, if it comes down to the will of God operating in our lives, how come God can still find fault with us? Well, if we stay close to the language of the Bible – and in a subject like this we really have to – then we'd have to say that being of a depraved mind and being dead in sins we had no ability of our own to come to Christ for salvation, so it had to be God's work. But at the same time we were held responsible. After all, didn't Christ describe unbelieving Jews of his day as being like chicks that wouldn't come to the mother hen? He was holding them accountable – responsible for their response.

We then find an almost irresistible urge to cry out: "But that's surely not fair!" (We have no ability, but God still holds us responsible!) And it's good that we feel like this, for again Paul by the Spirit anticipates exactly that kind of reaction – which reassures us that we must be on right lines after all! And this is where Paul parks the debate; for it's ridiculous to think of the mere clay of humanity criticising the divine potter. But does that mean God is responsible for people going to a lost eternity? Not at all! There can be no injustice with God. All the clay was spoilt, but that wasn't the Potter's fault; and he certainly has the right over the clay to do with some spoilt part of it something which that part deserves no more than the rest.

Well, we can even thank Pharaoh for his contribution to helping us strip away any remaining pride we may still have in thinking we made even the tiniest contribution to our salvation. More importantly, this impressive teaching of God's sovereignty provides us with the last word in complete assurance that once saved we can never be lost again. Let's not be foolish enough to expect we can fully get our heads round God and his perfect ways – but instead simply bow our hearts in worship! That's what Paul does in Romans 11:33. This is after he's traced God's sovereign dealings with the nation of Israel. They were set aside from the time of the cross, but after Christ returns for his Church (all believers between the cross and his return), God will again resume his dealings with Israel nationally. In chapter 10, Paul expresses a deep longing for his countrymen to be saved even as individuals during this mainly Gentile Church Age. And the basis for the free offer of the Gospel is that none of those who come to Christ for salvation will be rejected (John 6:37).

Questions for Further Study

1. It seems like an easy solution to a difficult problem to settle on God simply knowing in advance what is going to happen. How does the language of vv.18-23 address this?
2. Paul is adamant that there neither is, nor can be, injustice with God (v.14). What evidence does he present for this?
3. God's sovereignty does not preclude human freewill. How does Paul go on to tackle this (v.19ff)?
4. What are the implications of the language here in terms of 'the potter' and 'the clay'; and 'vessels of wrath' and 'vessels of mercy'?

7

Transformation

In the Apostle Paul's letters we always get doctrine first then comes the hinge. The hinge is the point where the letter turns from doctrine to practical exhortation. One pastor when asked to make his sermons more practical responded by saying that's precisely why he was being doctrinal! The teaching has to come first, and then the exhortation that applies it. That pastor was only following Paul's biblical example.

By the time Paul gets to chapter 12 of his letter to the Romans, he's covered the teaching of the Gospel under the headings of Condemnation, Justification, Sanctification, Glorification and Predestination. The hinge-point now comes at chapter 12 and lasts until near the end. This is where he deals with Transformation (chs.12-16): the transformation of our lives as a result of the Gospel. Here's how Paul begins this section, pivoting on the word "therefore":

"Therefore I urge you, brothers and sisters, by the mercies

of God, to present your bodies as a living and holy sacrifice, acceptable to God, which is your spiritual service of worship. And do not be conformed to this world, but be transformed by the renewing of your mind, so that you may prove what the will of God is, that which is good and acceptable and perfect" (Romans 12:1-3).

As we say, this is where Gospel truth "hits the tarmac" and gains traction in our lives. Praise God, the Gospel does change lives. Present your bodies as living sacrifices, Paul tells us. This is a return, a flashback, to what's been said earlier within the section of Romans we styled as Sanctification. In chapter 6: *"Just as you presented the parts of your body as slaves to impurity and to lawlessness, resulting in further lawlessness, so now present your body's parts as slaves to righteousness, resulting in sanctification"* (Romans 6:19).

In an earlier chapter, we commented on Augustine's conversion. There's a story about him following his conversion when he passed by one of his former mistresses on the street. Seeing him walk by she yelled after him, "Augustine, it is I!" Without turning back Augustine replied, "Yes, but it is no longer I!" His mind was now set on making no provision for the flesh (Romans 13:11). His sights were now set on living a sanctified life (Romans 6:19).

A recent convert was teased by one of his friends: "Do you really believe Jesus changed water into wine?" he asked. "What I do know is he can change beer into furniture," was his reply. With that he showed the man inside his newly furnished house. "I'm taking care of my family's needs now instead of wasting my money on excessive drinking," he explained. *"Be transformed,"* Paul writes. And next notice the following mention of the *"renewing of the mind."* For that's how the transformation in question comes about. What's the alternative if we don't allow our perspectives to be adjusted by absorbing the Bible's principles and values? It's only to have our thinking shaped instead by the influence of the world around us.

And this very much includes the pressure of our peers, and whatever is trending on Social Media – as when we instinctively and brainlessly "like" what others happen to be liking on Facebook, for example. The world is so good at squeezing us into its mould in the same way that a jelly takes the shape of whatever mould you choose to use when you pour it out and let it set. That means there are two moulds: the Word or the world. One or other of them is going to shape our thinking, and if our thinking gets shaped then so will our behaviours.

In the 1980s, according to a large (Gallup) survey in the United States, a very high percentage of people back then said they believed the Bible to be God's Word; and yet there was almost no difference between Christians and non-Christians when it came down to moral and ethical issues. Why? For all the then estimated 60 million Christian believers in the United States, the spirit of the age and a focus on worldly media had already shaped their thought patterns. The missing element was then – and remains to this day – our personal attention to spiritual transformation.

Today, in the west, it's as if a counter-Reformation has happened. Are we not in some sense seeing a reversal of what historically came to be known as the Protestant Reformation? The renewed interest in the Bible that took place in 16th century Europe once led to profound and beneficial developments in general society. Sadly, we see this progress all but reversed today, when our news items are populated with a great variety of decidedly unbiblical behaviours.

We might observe another contrasting example from history. In 18th century England, the revival that took place under John Wesley produced nationwide reformation. This is even confirmed by secular historians. They say it spared England of the fate that befell the French – that being a reference to the French Revolution. These historians were plainly acknowledging that before England had been impacted by the Word, it was a land of drugs, drunks and blood-sports.

As both the 16th century European Reformation and the 18th century English Revival demonstrate, whenever we allow our perceptions to be adjusted according to what we read in God's Word, our minds are renewed and this biblical kind of transformation in our behaviours takes place. Someone has warned us to beware of an untransformed mind. It's such a poor testimony. Transformation is what happens to the caterpillar as it morphs into a butterfly. It's the same word used for the transfiguration of the Lord's natural body in Matthew 17. He was glorified in his physical body then, and he will also be glorified in his mystical body, the Church. In practical terms, the makeover of our mind means affirming that God's will is best. That's what the end of verse three clarifies. The effects are seen within society. Imagine if most within society did the following:

"Bless those who persecute you; bless and do not curse. Rejoice with those who rejoice, and weep with those who weep. Be of the same mind toward one another; do not be haughty in mind, but associate with the lowly. Do not be wise in your own estimation. Never repay evil for evil to anyone. Respect what is right in the sight of all people. If possible, so far as it depends on you, be at peace with all people. Never take your own revenge ...

Every person is to be subject to the governing authorities. For there is no authority except from God, and those which exist are established by God. Therefore whoever resists authority has opposed the ordinance of God ... For rulers are not a cause of fear for good behavior, but for evil. Do you want to have no fear of authority? Do what is good and you will have praise from the same; for it is a servant of God to you for good. But if you do what is evil, be afraid; for it does not bear the sword for nothing; for it is a servant of God, an avenger who brings wrath on the one who practices evil.

Therefore it is necessary to be in subjection, not only because of wrath, but also for the sake of conscience. For because of this you also pay taxes, for rulers are servants of God, devoting themselves to this very thing. Pay to all what is due them: tax to whom tax is due; custom to whom custom; respect to whom respect; honor to whom honor" (Romans 12:14-13:7).

This is part of a transformed lifestyle -it's seen in respect for authority. How different this is from the spirit of the age we live in. The "yellow vests" protest movement started online in France and led to demonstrations that began on 17th November, 2018. It was motivated by rising fuel prices and a high cost of living. The country of Chile also has been rocked in recent times by unrest with riots, arson and looting as protesters demanded social reforms to provide better healthcare and education. The 2019 Hong Kong protests were part of an ongoing series of demonstrations triggered by concerns that Hong Kong residents would be subjected to the mainland Chinese legal system. When Spain's Supreme Court sentenced nine Catalan pro-independence leaders to jail for sedition, protesters set fires in the streets of Barcelona. In the UK, Extinction Rebellion (XR) attempted one of the biggest uprisings the UK has seen in modern times, trying to bring London to a standstill. More recently, there have been protests in Sri Lanka … the list could go on and on. But the person transformed by the Gospel will willingly be subject to all civil authorities, respecting them as established by God – even if he or she doesn't like a particular policy.

Another contrast seen in present-day society can be found in the area of tolerance or rather intolerance. It used to be the case that everyone's point of view was respected even if it was disagreed with. That's no longer the case. To express a particular biblical point of view nowadays, for example, may even in some places be regarded as committing a hate crime and brings criminal charges to bear. By contrast, in the outworking of the Gospel, Paul says in his 14th chapter:

> "Now accept the one who is weak in faith, but not to have quarrels over opinions. One person has faith that

49

he may eat all things, but the one who is weak eats only vegetables. The one who eats is not to regard with contempt the one who does not eat, and the one who does not eat is not to judge the one who eats, for God has accepted him ... One person values one day over another, another values every day the same. Each person must be fully convinced in his own mind... But as for you, why do you judge your brother or sister? ... each one of us will give an account of himself to God" (Romans 14:1-12).

Spiritual transformation is the process by which all the elements of self take on the character of the elements of Christ – so that we have his mind (1 Corinthians 2:16) and his affections (Philippians 1:8). It's both by putting off what's inconsistent with the life of our risen Lord, and by putting on what's consistent with it. Daily, God's Word in the power of his Spirit is to enter our mind and filter down into our heart and there shape our will to reform our very self. That's how we're to exchange the corrupted elements of self for those elements of his character; it's by renewing the spirit of our mind. It's the laying aside of the futile elements and the putting on of the new self as renewed in the image of God.

Questions for Further Study

1. When Paul begins his pivotal appeal by referencing 'the mercies of God', what do you think he's referring back to?
2. Which of the two moulds we identified in this chapter requires more diligent effort on our part if it is to shape our lives?
3. In what type of things should we be uncompromising; and

in what other type should we be prepared to show flexibility (see ch.14)?

4. What practical steps can we identify to progress our personal 'reformation'?

8

Conclusion

We now come to the last study in our series that has seen us working our way through the Apostle Paul's letter to the Romans. Naturally, we're calling it: Conclusion (ch.16). The conclusion of Paul's letter to the Romans contains another magnificent summary of the Gospel:

> *"Now to Him who is able to establish you according to my gospel and the preaching of Jesus Christ, according to the revelation of the mystery which has been kept secret for long ages past, but now is manifested, and by the Scriptures of the prophets, according to the command-ment of the eternal God, has been made known to all the nations, leading to obedience of faith; to the only wise God, through Jesus Christ, be the glory forever. Amen"* (Romans 16:25-27).

Again notice what Paul's Gospel is said to lead to: it's the obedience of faith. First and last in Romans, it's about the obedience of faith. Such a thing as "easy believe-ism" – just believe – wasn't known to Paul. That wasn't the essence of Paul's preaching. The Gospel, once accepted, should shape our whole life. As we saw from the previous section, it should transform our whole way of living.

Notice with me that this is not talking about obedience to the faith, but the obedience of faith. It's the obedience that charac-terizes faith and proceeds from it. Real faith is characterized by obedience. Yielding to the message is surrendering to Christ. It's striking that Paul concludes this letter to the Romans with an identical phrase to the one he introduces it with: *"the obedience of faith"* (1:5 and 16:26). He begins his letter by telling the Church of God in Rome that he'd *"received grace and apostleship to bring about the obedience of faith for the sake of* [Jesus'] *name among all the nations"*; and now he ends the letter by telling them that God's revelation in the *"prophetic writings"* (his Gospel plan) was *"to bring about the obedience of faith"* among all nations.

Faith, self-renouncing trust in Jesus Christ, is obedience to the gospel command to believe on the Lord Jesus Christ for salvation. That faith in Jesus Christ initiates a believer into a life of obedience to Jesus Christ. In concluding these studies on Paul's letter to the Romans, perhaps we can do no better than to look back again, over our shoulder as it were, at the ground we've covered – to gain a complete overview of this magnificent letter that so completely answers the question: "What is the Gospel?"

Paul has here set out for all time such a wonderfully orderly defence of the Gospel that it squarely faces up to and systemat-

53

ically defeats every conceivable objection that could be raised against the Gospel of Jesus Christ. This is about what God has done for us through his son, Jesus, and supremely what he did at the cross where Jesus died to pay the price of our rebellion, a rebellion that had alienated us from our creator, God.

To survey this glorious Gospel that's all of God's grace – grace being his favour that's totally undeserved by us – we've made use of the fact that it's previously been observed that there are eight main sections to this letter. We're now at the Conclusion, and it's a conclusion that follows on from other earlier sections of the letter that have been labelled as Condemnation, Justification, Sanctification, Glorification, Predestination and Transformation. And all these were, of course, introduced with the Introduction, giving eight sections in all. In the Introduction, Paul tells us the Gospel is divine as to both its source and subject. It is the Gospel of God concerning his son. And for sure, Paul's not ashamed of it. In fact, it's his only boast. He tells us it's the power of God for salvation to everyone who believes.

After the Introduction to the Gospel, Condemnation was the theme covered in the first major section of the Apostle Paul's letter to the Romans (1:18-3:20). It's a section that stretches from the middle of chapter one all the way until the middle of chapter three. The chief aim of this section is to show that all the world – the Jewish world as well as the Gentile world – was totally corrupted and guilty before a holy God whose anger burned against human sin. This is the bad news that defines the Gospel as being truly Good News.

If condemnation is about us being declared guilty before a

holy God whom we've offended by our rebellious attitude and behaviour against him, then justification is about us being declared righteous before God. It's about having a right standing before him, a right relationship with him. And that then meant the third section of Romans was on Justification, and it occupies us till we get to the end of chapter 5.

I just love how systematic the Apostle Paul is as the Spirit leads him in such an orderly way through these great themes of the Gospel. Not only do they follow on the one from the other, but when we came to look at Justification, we saw how Paul tackles it by first setting out its Instruction (3:21-26); and then its Implications (3:27-31); and finally, its Illustrations (chs. 4 & 5 dealing with Abraham and Adam).

Next came the fourth section of the Apostle Paul's letter to the Romans entitled 'Sanctification.' We saw it as being in two parts: in one sense it's already complete in Christ, but for the other part it's an ongoing process in Christian living. Paul's treatment of this topic of sanctification took us from the beginning of chapter 6 right through to someway down chapter 8. The start of chapter 6 is clearly dealing with sanctification – that is, holiness – because here Paul is responding to objectors who'd said to Paul: "we might as well go on sinning if we're assured of God's forgiveness!"

Having dealt with Condemnation, Justification and then Sanctification, we next came to Glorification, and that led us up to the end of Romans chapter 8. The future stage of glorification is when our sanctification will be complete in both senses. Remember, we've talked already about a once-for-all sanctification that God does for us when we receive Christ for salvation. But then there's also that which is our daily responsibility, and that is to cooperate with the promptings of the Spirit of God within us so that we live an increasingly holy life as far as our Christian behaviour is concerned. We are holy, so we've now got to become holy! A lot of the teaching of the New Testament is about believers on the Lord Jesus becoming what they already are. That is, becoming in practical terms day to day the same as God already sees us as being in Christ. It's catching up with reality. When in the future we stand with Christ in glory, we'll have fully become in every sense what we truly already have been by grace in Christ from the time of our salvation.

I was illustrating this at a summer Bible camp this year. I had one person represent Jesus Christ, while another - at the totally opposite side of the room - was representing Adolf Hitler. Then I called for another lad to represent the Apostle Paul, the godly writer of this letter to the Romans. At first, I placed him halfway between the first two persons, halfway on the scale between the extremes we've mentioned. I asked the audience if they thought I should be moving Paul nearer to Jesus or nearer to Hitler. Some thought I should lead him higher up the scale, closer to the person representing Jesus. But then I moved him in the opposite direction until he was standing right next to Hitler. This certainly surprised some. Surely, there exists a big difference between Hitler and the Apostle Paul!

There certainly does – but the object of the demonstration was to illustrate that there is an incomparably bigger difference between Jesus and Paul than there is between Paul and Hitler. God is holy - he is totally other than we are in that respect.

But when we who have trusted in Christ alone for salvation are finally glorified, we will be as close to being like Christ as it's possible for any creature to be. This is the ultimate goal of our sanctification and transformation.

Well, back to our Romans review, for chapters 9 through 11 we had the heading Predestination (or Election). This is the deepest truth of the Gospel, but one that finds an echo in John chapter 6 and Ephesians chapter 1. We were chosen to become holy before time ever began!

So, by the time Paul gets to chapter 12 of his letter to the Romans, he's covered the teaching of the Gospel under the headings of Condemnation, Justification, Sanctification, Glorification and Predestination. The hinge-point, we said, came at chapter 12 and lasts until near the end. This is where he deals with Transformation (chs.12-15) - the transformation of our lives as a result of the Gospel. This section on application of all the truth that's gone before is clearly signalled by the first word of chapter 12 usually being found to be the word "therefore."

May God help us very ordinary people (exactly like the 24 persons named in the Conclusion of this letter) to live out such extraordinary Good News! To God be all the glory!

Questions for Further Study

1. How would you sum up the Gospel in some way that captures the sense of vv.25-27?
2. It was stated that a lot of New Testament teaching amounts to 'becoming what we already are.' Holiness was one

57

example. Can you give some others?

3. An illustration was shared concerning how we relate to Christ (or Hitler) on the scale of holiness. Did anything surprise you there? If so, how?

4. In what way does it seem appropriate that Paul ends by naming and commenting on some quite ordinary persons in the greetings he wished to be conveyed?

About the Author

Born and educated in Scotland, Brian worked as a government scientist until God called him into full-time Christian ministry on behalf of the Churches of God (www.churchesofgod.info). His voice has been heard on Search For Truth radio broadcasts for 40 years (visit www.searchfortruth.podbean.com) during which time he has been an itinerant Bible teacher throughout the UK. His evangelical and missionary work outside the UK is primarily in Belgium, The Philippines and South East Central Africa. He is married to Rosemary, with a son and daughter.

More Books from Brian Johnston

The Character of Christ in Paul's Letters

Brian explores how the apostle Paul sought to defend himself against criticism in his letters, and in particularly in 2 Corinthians, by looking at various aspects of the person and ministry of Jesus that he sought to emulate:

- Chapter 1: The Love of Christ
- Chapter 2: The Obedience of Christ
- Chapter 3: The Meekness of Christ
- Chapter 4: The Gentleness of Christ
- Chapter 5: The Purity of Christ
- Chapter 6: The Dignity of Christ
- Chapter 7: The Steadfastness or Patience of Christ
- Chapter 8: The Humility of Christ
- Chapter 9: The Kindness and Compassion of Christ
- Chapter 10: The Faithfulness of Christ

Finding Christ in the Old Testament

"They said to one another, 'Were our hearts not burning within us when He was speaking to us on the road, while He was explaining the Scriptures to us?'" *(Lk.24:27:32)* Burning hearts -

the inevitable result of having the Bible explained so it all begins to make sense and the person and work of Christ, its central character, comes into sharper focus. Brian used to think it would be wonderful to know what Old Testament incidents, symbols and themes the Lord unpacked for them. The way to do it seems obvious to him now! Wouldn't they be the same things that he and his Apostles spoke about – things that were later recorded and expounded in the New Testament? This book is the result of that thought process and picks up on these themes using as near as possible the order in which we encounter them in the Old Testament, including:

- Born of a Woman (Galatians 4:4)
- The Type of Him Who Was to Come (Romans 5:14)
- The Only Begotten Son (Hebrews 11:17-19)
- Christ Our Passover (1 Corinthians 5:7)
- The Bread That Came Out of Heaven (John 6:51)
- Sacrifice and Offering (Hebrews 10:5) & The Blood of Goats and Bulls (Hebrews 9:13)
- The Firstfruits
- The Ashes of a (Red) Heifer (Hebrews 9:13)
- The Bronze Serpent
- The King-Priest
- The Suffering Servant (1 Peter 2:24)
- Son of Man (Matthew 26:62)
- The Sign of Jonah (Matthew 12:39)

First Corinthians - Nothing But Christ Crucified

Brian unpacks one of the most important letters in the New Testament, which gives us important teaching on such topics as spiritual gifts, the body of Christ, church discipline and leadership, head coverings, the Breaking of Bread and, most importantly, the powerful wisdom of God displayed through the crucified Christ! An ideal companion commentary to any study of the epistle.

- Chapter 1: The Ultimate Truth is Cross-Centred
- Chapter 2: The Scandal to End All Scandals
- Chapter 3: God's Deepest Secrets Revealed
- Chapter 4: Working Collectively But Individually Accountable
- Chapter 5: Biblical Church Discipline
- Chapter 6: Glorifying God With Our Body
- Chapter 7: Things Associated With Married Life
- Chapter 8: Clear Conscience And Kind Consideration
- Chapter 9: Integrity In Serving The Lord
- Chapter 10: A Special Type Of Warning
- Chapter 11: Giving All The Glory To God
- Chapter 12: A Serious Eating Disorder
- Chapter 13: There's Unity In Diversity
- Chapter 14: The More Excellent Way
- Chapter 15: When To Speak And When Be Silent
- Chapter 16: The Ultimate Test Of Christianity

About Hayes Press

Hayes Press (www.hayespress.org) is a registered charity in the United Kingdom, whose primary mission is to disseminate the Word of God, mainly through literature. It is one of the largest distributors of gospel tracts and leaflets in the United Kingdom, with over 100 titles and many thousands dispatched annually. In addition to paperbacks and eBooks, Hayes Press also publishes Plus Eagles' Wings, a fun and educational Bible magazine for children, and Golden Bells, a popular daily Bible reading calendar in a wall/desk format.

If you would like to contact Hayes Press, there are a number of ways you can do so:

By mail: c/o The Barn, Flaxlands, Royal Wootton Bassett, Wiltshire, UK SN4 8DY

By phone: 01793 850598

By eMail: info@hayespress.org

via Facebook: www.facebook.com/hayespress.org

www.ingramcontent.com/pod-product-compliance
Lightning Source LLC
Chambersburg PA
CBHW071850020426
42331CB00007B/1947